How to be evil

Since the launch of **Delayed Gratification** magazine in January 2011, a Machiavellian doodle known simply as Evil Stick Man has shared his devious get-rich-quick schemes with readers each issue, from dodging tax and rigging polls to starting currency wars and shaking down online music services.

As a tribute to Evil Stick Man, we've pulled together his greatest scams into this compendium of skulduggery. While we cannot condone his unscrupulous behaviour, we do hope you enjoy his step by step, highly lucrative guide to How to be evil.

Rob and Marcus
Editors
Delayed Gratification
slow-journalism.com

GW00707707

How to be evil

Words
Rob Orchard, Marcus
Webb, Loes Witschge,
Oli Rahman, Alex Hacillo

Illustrations
Christian Tate

Book design
Christian Tate, Vanessa
Arnaud, Ro Atkins

Printing and binding
Westdale Press Ltd.

THE SLOW JOURNALISM COMPANY
LAST TO BREAKING NEWS

● Contents

(1)

How to manipulate a search engine

❶ Find a client whose business depends on being high in search engine rankings and for whom each step up in the rankings represents a large increase in potential revenue.

❷ Agree to increase their ranking for a major fee, with special bonuses if you get them in the top three results for key search terms.

❸ Set up a bot to spider through the websites of major news and cultural organisations across the world looking for outward links to sites which are now defunct.

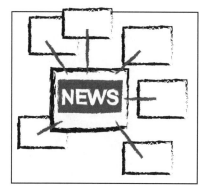

❹ Isolate those sites which have only recently become defunct, so that search engines have not had a chance to assess them as such. Purchase the URLs for these sites.

❺ You now own a set of websites which have a high credibility ranking with search engines thanks to being linked to by major news and cultural organisations. Any links from these sites will also carry additional credibility.

❻ Pay a boiler room of writers in a developing country to start writing dozens of blog entries a day on the subject matter covered by your client's business. They do not have to be experts on the subject.

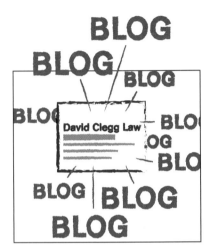

❼ Post these blog entries on your websites and include multiple links to your client's site.

❽ The host of new, regularly posted links from credible sites will make your client's site rise in the rankings. Collect your payment. Repeat steps ❶ to ❽ .

❾ You are now rich. Pay David Attenborough to follow you around and narrate your every move in an excited whisper.

2

How to make cold hard cash from cold callers

❶ Set up a premium rate phone number which gives you a large one-off payment and per-minute fee for each call received.

❷ Update your bank, utilities providers, pay-TV company and insurers with your new premium rate phone number.

❸ Sign up for every free quote callback service you see advertised online. Give your number and details freely to companies who stop you in the street.

❹ Get your landline to forward to a mobile headset. Start receiving calls.

❺ Begin each call by making the caller listen to you practising "Chopsticks" on the piano.

❻ Keep the salespeople talking for as long as possible by speaking slowly, getting them to repeat everything and asking them to spell "PPI". Experiment with a series of different accents.

❼ Field calls while making tea, reading Russian novels or playing arpeggios. If you get bored, buy a parrot and train it to say "mmm hmmm" and "sounds good!" at random intervals.

❽ When an automated robot calls with a pre-recorded sales message, take a well-earned break from your headset and perfect your Beethoven sonata.

❾ You are now rich. Buy your way on to the bill at the Last Night of the Proms.

(3)

How to work a crypto-currency scam

❶ Browse meme aggregation websites to find a burgeoning meme which you can use to create a mascot and name for your currency.

❷ Make your new currency through a coin creation service. Use your new mascot as the logo.

❸ Pay a hacker to use Trojan software to get high-powered computers in countries around the world to start mining your currency without their owners' knowledge.

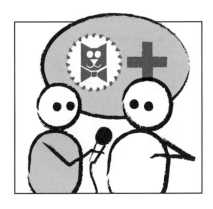

❹ Get the hacker to bounce the currency around between the computers in a series of false transactions, to give the impression of multi-user activity whilst maintaining control of all new coins mined. Build up a solid stash.

❺ Promote your currency to the press, emphasising its whimsical mascot and claiming it's the new Bitcoin. Bored students will market your currency while spreading the meme and early adopters will mine it, kickstarting its growth.

❻ Release growth stats to the press. Give interviews to technology publications claiming that your crypto-currency is now a serious endeavour. Offer coins to websites that allow people to use it for transactions.

❼ Large mining pools and speculators will begin to engage with your crypto-currency. Release still bigger growth figures to the press.

❽ Watch as a speculative bubble develops, fueled by hype, greed and the irresistible appeal of online memes. Quietly sell your coins at its height.

❾ You are now rich. Lobby the Bank of England to put your face on the new five pound note.

(4)

How to exploit a walk of fame

 ❶ Approach the local council in a rundown but central area of a major city, ideally in an important market for the entertainment industry.

 ❷ Posing as a concerned citizen, offer to take over the maintenance of a major street for a third of the current cost, but insist on a long-term deal.

 ❸ Announce that you will be launching the city's version of the Hollywood Walk Of Fame on the street.

❹ Invite celebrity A to be honoured with a star. Charge only a minimal fee for upkeep but insist that celebrity A must attend the unveiling.

❺ Unveil the new star with a grand ceremony, timed to coincide with the celebrity's latest product release. Invite the press, giving the celebrity maximum exposure.

❻ Repeat steps ❹ to ❺ with other major and minor celebrities. Watch your street become a tourist attraction.

❼ Contact celebrity A's agent to tell them you need to increase the maintenance fee significantly. If the agent refuses to pay, have their client's star publicly removed and destroyed with journalists present.

❽ Continue to collect vastly inflated fees from agents worried about bad publicity. Occasionally pay a street cleaner to sweep up.

❾ You are now rich. Pay for a shot for shot remake of 'The Sound Of Music', with you playing every role. Watch it in your own private cinema every bank holiday.

(5)

How to pull off a transfer coup

❶ Set yourself up as an agent. Contract two unsigned strikers, stipulating you will get 20 percent of all their transfer fees. Oversee sale of Player A to Club X and Player B to Club Y. Pocket your 20 percent.

❷ Wait six months. Place an anonymous tip to a major sports channel that the manager of Club X is tracking Player B. Watch it get released as 'breaking news'.

❸ Get a tame journalist to ask the manager of Club X whether he is a fan of Player B. Watch him say yes (they never say no).

❹ Get the tame journalist to ask Player B if he would be flattered to play for Club X. Watch him say yes (they never say no).

❺ Point out to Player A that his club appear to be openly courting Player B, who plays in the same position as him. Player A will now tweet something stupid. Player B will respond in kind.

❻ Turn all conversations with journalists to the "war" between clubs X and Y over players A and B.

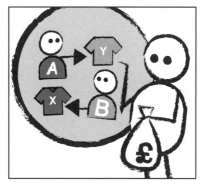

❼ Enjoy ensuing media storm during which players demand "dream move", fans demand "dream signing" and the cost of the players rises.

❽ Oversee sales of Player A to Club Y and Player B to Club X. Pocket your fee. Repeat steps ❶ to ❽ every six months.

❾ You are now rich. Pay to have your face added to Mount Rushmore.

6

How to become an IT millionaire

❶ Place an advert on a jobs website, advertising for high level IT staff and asking applicants to send in CVs.

❷ Pick the most impressive CV, switch the applicant's personal data for your own, and change the company names cited for your own, made-up names (include the word "Solutions" as much as possible). Leave all the job title and experience information.

❸ Sign up to a reference provider, who for a small monthly fee will create websites and phone numbers for your made-up companies and provide fabricated references from them as well as fielding calls from potential employers.

❹ Apply for high level remote-working IT jobs until you secure one on the basis of your CV and references.

❺ Set up a proxy server at your home address.

❻ Hire an IT graduate in a developing nation to do your job for you, using your login codes, and working through the proxy server so as not to raise any alarm over foreign IP addresses. Pay them a third of your salary.

❼ Watch cat videos.

❽ Repeat steps **❹** to **❼** until you have a whole string of high paid, farmed-out jobs.

❾ You are now rich. Pay Michael Flatley to come round to your house and teach you the Riverdance.

(7)

How to be a
patent troll

❶ Find a tech start-up, Company A, run by naive geeks with a patented product they are yet to produce. Lend them money for swanky offices and offer free legal advice to get them going.

❷ Instruct your lawyers to do little and take their time. Having done nothing to advance the business for six months, demand the repayment of the loan, forcing the company into bankruptcy.

❸ Buy up the now-bankrupt company for a pittance. Do nothing with the company, produce nothing, employ nobody.

❹ Monitor the tech news for launches similar to Company A's patented product. Keep a particular eye on the companies who have employed the heartbroken former employees of Company A.

❺ When Company B announces the launch of a similar product, file a perfunctory infringement complaint against it.

❻ A court will issue a mutual injunction, which will shut down the manufacturing and other business operations of Company B until the case is settled. This injunction will also stop you producing the products that you aren't producing.

❼ Instruct your lawyers to continue to do little and take their time, stalling the legal process as much as possible.

❽ Without income and with no court date in sight, Company B will either settle out of court (proceed to ❾) or file for bankruptcy (return to ❸).

❾ You are now rich. Pay Celine Dion to perform a private concert for you. Don't turn up.

8

How to besmirch a political reputation

❶ Think of something shocking and horrible (Horrible Thing A).

❷ Think of something even worse (Horrible Thing A+).

❸ After securing a hefty fee from your politician client, use intermediaries to contact a techno geek who hates your client's political opponent but has no identifiable link to you.

❹ Get the geek to set up Site A, a simple website whose text defines your client's political opponent's surname as being synonymous with Horrible Thing A+. Ensure metadata are correct so it is indexed.

❺ Using intermediaries, encourage politically likeminded bloggers across the world to place mentions of your client's political opponent in their blogs with hyperlinks to Site A. The site will rise higher in the search rankings with every link.

❻ Get your techno geek to employ spamdexing techniques on Site A to help it rise even further in the search rankings. Soon it will be on the first page of results.

❼ Get your PR people to place untraceable stories in the mainstream media about the rise of Site A, making it rise still further in the search rankings. Then get them to put references to the scandal in your opponent's Wikipedia page.

❽ Go on TV to say how appalled you are that your client's political opponent has been identified with Horrible Thing A+, thereby drawing additional attention to the link and helping Site A hit the top of the rankings. Collect a bonus fee from your client.

❾ Your client's opponent will spend vast sums to push Site A off the search rankings top spot. They will forever be associated with Horrible Thing A+. Repeat steps ❶ to ❽ for other clients. You are now rich. Launch your own line of designer whisky.

9

How to leave a currency union

❶ Become prime minister. Meet in secret with the head of your national bank and identify an upcoming bank holiday on which to leave your joint currency A and revert to your former national currency B.

❷ Do not tell anyone else. If word got out, your countrymen would immediately rush to take out their life savings in currency A, creating a huge run on the banks and leading to the collapse of civil society.

❸ Get your finance minister consistently and publicly to ridicule the notion that your country might leave the currency union, and to emphasise how vital the union and your currency partners are.

❹ Order hundreds of millions of bank notes denominated in currency B from government printers in friendly and discreet dictatorship D. Call the currency 'New Currency B' and illustrate the notes with patriotic scenes.

❺ Liquidate your personal assets and transfer the funds to an offshore bank account denominated in stable currency C. Place 80 per cent of your savings into an inverse exchange-traded fund that bets against the value of joint currency A.

❻ On the chosen bank holiday, have all bank accounts re-denominated in New Currency B, and all cash machines filled with New Currency B bank notes.

❼ Appear on TV to announce the switchover, the repudiation of all national debts and the lowering of nominal interest rates to zero per cent. Blame your currency partners and imply a conspiracy between them and your finance minister. Sack your finance minister live on air.

❽ Reopen the banks and float New Currency B. Its value will drop like a stone, giving a huge boost to your export market. Currency A will undergo a huge dip too: cash in your inverse exchange-traded fund at its low point. You are now rich.

❾ If your country is not destroyed by hyperinflation, growth should pick up within a few months. If it does, stay on as PM and, in a few years, renegotiate entry to financial markets by paying back some of the repudiated debt. If it doesn't, leave and start a new life in dictatorship D.

10

How to
rig a poll

❶ Secure secret funding from the campaign for Candidate A to produce a poll in their favour. Set up a polling company with a name which suggests patriotism and impartiality. Finance it through a shell company.

❷ Skew the selection of poll participants. Carry out your poll in cities or regions where Candidate A has the most support. Extrapolate from these results to represent the whole country.

❸ If young people are unlikely to support Candidate A, carry out the poll through landline calls. If they are likely to support Candidate A, carry out the poll online and link responses to social media incentives.

❹ Your key question should be "Given that X, do you agree that candidate A deserves to win?", where X is information which supports your cause.
You will not publish the first part of the question in the final results.

❺ If your case is strengthened by the state of the economy, ask a series of questions about it before posing your key question. You will not publish these questions in the final results.

❻ Use polling agents with a regional accent associated with trustworthiness: they will help sway participants to give a positive answer to your key question.

❼ Conduct your poll at a time when Candidate A is going through a bounce in popularity. Release the poll result several weeks later when Candidate A is going through a dip in popularity, so it looks like they are doing well even in adversity.

❽ Only include the responses to the key question in the release of your poll data. Factor in an additional margin of error to the result that works in your favour. Disseminate the outcome of the poll widely through the media.

❾ Collect a payoff from Candidate A. Secure secret funding from the campaign of Candidate B, then work through steps ❶ to ❽ on their behalf. You are now rich. Pay Damien Hirst to make a model of your skull out of diamonds.

11

How to start
a gold farm

❶ Recruit an anonymous group of anarchy-minded geeks on games forums. Form an alliance in an MMOG (Massively Multiplayer Online Game) and start buying up virtual minerals and armoured vehicles.

❷ Having cornered as much of the virtual mineral market as possible, get your alliance to start blowing up virtual mines and mineral dumps, thus inflating the value of your own holding.

❸ Sell your minerals and use the credits to invest in more sophisticated attack vehicles. Get your team to blow up as many of other players' attack vehicles as possible, inflating the value of your own.

④ Identify a war taking place in the MMOG, and play the two sides off against one another, offering to arm each side against the other. Sell your virtual attack vehicles to the highest bidder for credits.

⑤ Sell your MMOG credits to time-poor, cash-rich gamers on MMOG forums in return for real world money.

⑥ Dump your online crew and invest your real world cash in a "gold farm" – a boiler room of low-paid, non-unionised workers in a foreign country. Equip them with second-hand games consoles.

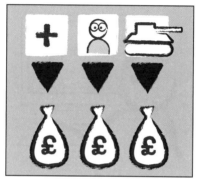

🔘 Get your workers to toil 12 hours a day "grinding" MMOGs, building up game credits, enhanced avatars and saleable virtual weapons.

🔘 Sell these credits, avatars and weapons to gamers for real money. Get more money for taking their login details and getting your gold farmers to take them to the next level of games. Repeat steps 🔘 to 🔘.

🔘 You are now rich. Buy a house on the moon.

12

How to run a penny stock pump and dump

❶ Identify a failing, low profile, low market capitalisation target company in country A. Its low capitalisation will mean it isn't listed on a stock exchange – so there will be little independent information available about it.

❷ Spend 80% of your capital for this project buying a huge amount of the target company's stock through a compromised brokerage firm in country B.

❸ Commission a boiler room of telemarketers in low-regulation country C to cold call thousands of small brokerage firms across the world and talk up the target company.

❹ Get a teenage tech geek to send an e-blast recommending investment in the target company to millions of email addresses across the world through a network of hacked botnet computers.

❺ Using a proxy host in country D to disguise your IP address, fill the forums of share-tipping websites with rumours that a major announcement is to be made by the target company's board about a revolutionary new product launch.

❻ The share price of the target company will start to rise steeply as its stock is snapped up. Use your telemarketing, spamming and forums teams to spread the news of this rise.

❼ Spend the remaining 20% of your project capital in buying a further tranche of shares in the target company, making the price leap. Repeat point ❻ .

❽ Day traders, sensing an easy win, will start to pile in. The share price of the target company will start to rise even more precipitously.

❾ Sell all your stock in the target company at a huge profit. You are now rich. Send a fruit basket and a cryptic note to the CEO of the target company. Buy that château you've had your eye on.

13

How to cash in on high frequency trading

❶ Find a financial market with lousy regulatory authorities and move there.

❷ Buy an office as close as possible to the point where the internet line exits the stock exchange. It is key that nobody can get closer. A shed would work just fine.

❸ Buy a powerful computer. Install some high frequency trading software on it. Hook it up to the same fibre-optic line used by the stock exchange.

❹ Your computer will wait for a mutual fund to release blue chip stock through the exchange. Being right next to the exchange building means your computer will get this info nanoseconds before anyone else. You can play with a yo-yo.

❺ The release of stock will cause its price to dip momentarily, only to correct seconds later. At the bottom of this dip the programme on your computer will buy the stock on credit, selling it the moment the price bounces back.

❻ Make a cup of tea (your computer can process up to 900,000 transactions in this time), have a 45-minute nap (13,500,000 transactions), watch 'Wolf of Wall Street' (54,000,000 transactions). Each transaction will bring a small profit.

❼ Use your profits to expand your office and install further data lines in your building. Rent these to other like-minded 'traders' for exorbitant amounts of money.

❽ Watch as millions of dollars are extracted from the market with not a cent of value added.

❾ You are now rich. Buy Frans Hals's 'The Laughing Cavalier'. Replace his face with your own. Frowning.

14

How to mastermind a ghost game

① Identify bookmakers who employ data scouts to report on key events during a match in the absence of live television coverage or video streaming. Open online accounts with all of them.

② Approach a data scout in City X, a second-tier city in a country where there's an interest in football but no televised games. Scouts are usually low-paid and provide info to a number of bookies.

③ Bribe the scout to add in a brief delay when reporting vital moments in the game, informing you of what's happening first. Capitalise on in-play odds by betting on key moments during the lag.

④ Use your new found Nostradamus skills to amass a stockpile of cash. Pay a hacker to insert a made-up fixture in City X into the info that sports data companies provide to the bookmaking industry.

⑤ Get your data scout to cover the non-existent game. Make them begin the live coverage with Team B having a player sent off and team A taking a healthy lead.

⑥ As odds on a Team B victory lengthen, get the scout to report the conceding of more goals, the sending off of two more players and the arrest of the manager for biting an official.

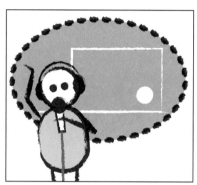

❼ As the game enters the final five minutes and the odds reach ridiculous proportions, bet heavily on Team B across all your bookmakers.

❽ Have your data scout report an amazing comeback for team B. Collect your winnings. Repeat steps ❹ to ❽ until your data scout is rumbled.

❾ You are now rich. Bribe FIFA to move the 2022 World Cup to the North Pole. Insist that players wear shorts.

15

How to
astroturf a campaign

① Set up a boiler room full of computers in a foreign jurisdiction with cheap labour, lax laws on unfair commercial practices and no links to your campaign or product.

② Load the computers with software that creates "sockpuppets" – multiple virtual online identities, with their own names, emails and social media accounts.

③ For the next few months these accounts will retweet links, post feeds on sites, update profiles etc, to make it look as though they are being run by real, active humans.

④ Staff your boiler room with low-paid techies. Get them to start posting thousands of positive online messages about your campaign or product using their pre-aged multiple personas and attacking the online posts of competitors/groups opposed to your campaign.

⑤ Back in your home country, set up a company in the capital city and name it using words which connote independence, public interest and a groundswell of support: "Network", "Research", "Foundation" and "Alliance" are all good.

⑥ Staff the company with a small team of former journalists who will commission surveys and reports from minor-league academics showing how much the public approves of your campaign or product and how much they disapprove of those of your competitors.

⑦ Co-opt a tame scientist/economist (for legitimacy) and a folksy, salt-of-the-earth character (for authenticity) as spokespeople and get them as many media interviews as possible. A couple of celebrity endorsements will also help.

⑧ Get the boiler room team to flood the online forums of media groups with messages of support for your campaign or product after every appearance by your spokespeople. Send "cease and desist" legal letters to critical bloggers.

⑨ Watch as your campaign or product attains success and exposure completely out of proportion to its actual levels of popular support. You are now rich. Treat yourself to a fancy cocktail with a platinum umbrella in it.

How to avoid paying corporation tax

16

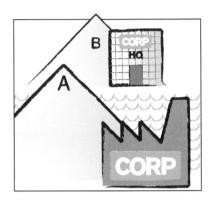

❶ Move your company's headquarters from Country A, your high-tax birthplace, to Country B, an accessible European nation with low levels of corporation tax.

❷ Set up a shell company in Country C – a Caribbean island with low or no levels of corporation tax. Do not visit the company, employ any staff or produce any goods or services.

❸ Put the rights to your brand under the legal ownership of the shell company. Get the shell company to charge your main operation large sums to use its own name and brand identity. Pay these charges: this money is now untaxable.

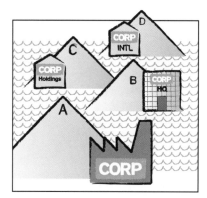

④ Your shareholders will reward you with a handsome raise and make "thumbs up" signs at you. Buy yourself a Porsche.

⑤ Problem: you can't funnel the remainder of the company's profit directly from Country B to Country C without incurring tax. Solution part one: set up a second shell company in Country D. Do not visit it, employ any staff or produce any goods or services.

⑥ Solution part two: send all payments which come in to Country B immediately on to your company in Country D, which has accommodating tax laws for onward transfers to Country C. Your shareholders will welcome you to the AGM with a standing ovation. Treat yourself to a nice yacht.

❼ Transfer your shares in all companies to your husband, wife or partner. Move them to Country E – which levies no income tax on individuals – for one whole tax year. They are now classed as "non-resident for tax purposes" in Country A.

❽ Take out a company loan and use it to help fund a large dividend to all the shareholders, including your partner. Offset the interest payable on the loan against your annual profits when calculating your corporation tax in Country A. Accept another raise from the board.

❾ You are now rich. Take a celebratory flight to Country E in your new golden helicopter.

17

How to make a killing
from a smoking ban

❶ Buy a bar in a city which has recently introduced a smoking ban and where stripping is illegal.

❷ Examine the clauses of the smoking ban relating to smoking and the arts. You will find an exemption that states that smoking indoors is permitted if you are an actor in a play, and your character smokes.

❸ Declare that your bar is staging a continuous live performance. Hand all customers stage directions giving them the role of 'smoking patron' and ask them to improvise conversation while smoking. Stream the event live online.

④ Watch as your bar swells with 'actors' during the cold winter months. Use the money raised to buy a second bar nearby.

⑤ Examine the clauses of the ban on public nudity relating to the arts. You will find a subsection that states that public nudity is permitted for art classes.

⑥ Open your second bar. Hire people to pose on the stage naked.

❼ Hand every patron entering the bar a sketch pad and pencil and ask them to absorb the naked form in front of them before capturing it on paper.

❽ Watch as your bar fills year round with 'artists'. Repeat stages ❶ to ❼ in a series of different cities.

❾ You are now rich. Pay to have a giant wall built around Donald Trump.

18

How to shake down a music service

① Create an enigmatic band name which alludes to your plan, e.g. "The Nothing".

② Record ten tracks of silence, each around 30 seconds long. Use the names of existing songs (e.g. "It's Oh So Quiet") so some people will think that they are covers.

③ Sign up to a band aggregator service that distributes to music streaming services around the world. Submit the album to any other streaming sites you can find.

④ Set up Facebook, Twitter and Instagram accounts for your band. Create a buzz by spreading rumours that it's the new, undercover project of an enigmatic music producer with a loyal army of superfans. Watch your social media following soar.

⑤ Anonymously email music journalists and bloggers across the globe. Tip each of them off that a different artist or producer is behind the project and that the silent album is a ruse to fund a free global tour. Watch the rumour mill kick into top gear.

⑥ Record a YouTube clip asking your fans to play your silent album on loop on music streaming services while they sleep to fund the free tour. Wear a mask and distort your voice to remain anonymous.

⑦ Spread the clip through your social media channels. Post your free tour dates online. Wait for your newly acquired fanbase to listen to your "songs" millions of times, earning you a tiny amount each time.

⑧ Cancel your free tour, citing artistic differences with yourself. Disappear into anonymity.

⑨ You are now rich. Pay to reform The Beatles with you replacing both John and George. Don't invite Ringo.

(19)

How to start a
currency war

❶ Become prime minister of nation A. Identify competitor nation B, in whose markets you wish to stimulate demand for your products.

❷ Start buying large quantities of their currency on the international markets. Stockpile it.

❸ Watch as their currency becomes stronger against your own currency, thereby making your products more affordable in their market. Sales of your nation's products should now increase.

❹ Buy more of your competitor's currency. Stockpile it. Watch your sales increase still further, while sales of your competitor's products in your own country decrease.

❺ Your competitor should now be angry.

❻ Your competitor may demand that you re-value your currency in the interests of free trade. They may hint at tariffs and sanctions should you refuse.

❼ Refuse. Your competitor may now start to print money, to flood the market and bring down the value of their currency.

❽ Respond by buying and stockpiling more of your competitor's currency. Your competitor may now redouble their money printing – or offer you a sizeable personal bribe to stop.

❾ If you take the bribe and stop the currency war, congratulations! You are now rich. If not, simply enjoy watching the global economy spiral out of control.